BURN BABY BURN

POEMS

Roger Aplon

First Edition: 2022
Rs. 200/-

Cyberwit.net
HIG 45 Kaushambi Kunj, Kalindipuram
Allahabad - 211011 (U.P.) India
http://www.cyberwit.net
Tel: +(91) 9415091004
E-mail: info@cyberwit.net

Printed at Vcore Connect LLP.

Dedicated To

Debra

Who's stood with me
Even through the tough times

Contents

Burn Baby Burn

Our house is on fire. The Amazon, the lungs of our planet that produces 20% of our oxygen, is on fire."

Emmanuel Macron, President of France
August 22, 2019

Drive business-for-business-sake from this magnificent & healing expanse. Replant & sustain what was given you in trust . . . for all who breathe.

Anonymous
October 2019

**

Hear It? *Burn-Baby-Burn*: That insidious cry of Brazil's President Jair Bolsonaro & his minions of ranchers, farmers, loggers & miners, those who ignore

the lost chatter of the Brown-Throated Sloth, the eerie cry of the Howler Monkey, the hiss & growl of the resplendent Jaguar, ignore

the loss of the Scarlet Macaw, the Blue Poison-dart Frog & Yes. the human families that have lived among these trees & vines for centuries.

As the planet's temperature rises for want of CO_2 relief, this massive forest that sucks up that CO_2 & gives us oxygen is being dismantled, set afire & destroyed.

Burn Baby Burn rouses the irresponsible & incendiary – driven by greed they ignite the day – arouse the night / where death waits / in the wings.

This forest is fundamental – To our planet & For Its people.   Brazil.   Yes

Brazil
You Must Act   Stop
This incendiary
Holocaust

*

Thank You!

To All Those Who've Devoted Themselves To The Survival Of Our Endangered Planet

"Lest We Forget"

Dead Pigeon

I weep for my country, for its eagerness to kill & to maim in the name of freedom

from fear

I challenge my country

to resurrect her promises of fealty to colleagues – to challenge those who hide in isolation

& deny these promises

*

There's a dead pigeon underfoot for each one swimming in your pot. There's a dragon breathing fire in each corner of the blind man's dream.

They come from the center of the earth trailing the dried skin & bones of those soldiers left behind.

There's no dance of the lily & the rose, no crown of laurel fitted like scales to protect the king's guard.

All that's ever left are the ashes & the drums & the wailing from the hills where mothers have gone to wash the dead.

Afghanistan 2019

20 years & no end in sight

Green Tea & Tulips

February warns of more victims & the ritual of retribution

The bearer of the cup cannot be trusted.
Who will nurture the buds of spring?

This is the way of the blind among us.
Will no one stand to open the gates?

The old table's been split in two.
Who will wipe the widow's tears?

There's been sleet & a hard rain for weeks.
Will a new face appear at the door?

We're poised at the edge of the hole we've dug.
Who will drive the madman from the house?

[war in Iraq escalates]

In August

The bodies float by. It's hot. 110. We've been walking the riverbank harvesting crayfish. Watching.

They're from the north, somewhere behind the trees. Vultures & the stench precede them. A woman in white

signals from the cliffs above. She waves a yellow flag imprinted with the image of a human skull.

The drumming has begun in earnest. Masked dancers appear in the guise of goat & antelope.

Last night, men arrived from the south. They unloaded an army of clay figurines, machetes & gin,

moved all & themselves to the cave reserved for the whores, their kids & the reaper of bones.

Jackie notices the bluesy wail of a harmonica. Unlikely but true, here, where the known world ends.

We see him then, across the river, tall & regal in his bright red robes & golden turban, blowing in the key of D.

The priests come next, followed by the builders of ships & temples. They cross on the bodies

trapped in mounds against the fallen trees, where the river bends & herons nest. Above,

framed against the sky, the metal skeleton of the guillotine shimmers in the waning light.

Tonight is the night we've come to anticipate, when the house is swept clean (*as the people say*),

when truth is extracted from those who wait, when those who cannot
remember are slaughtered, when

why we've come is explained & the toll we must pay is collected.
There's no way to amend history or

     the stink of the dead

        floating

           out of sight

             around the bend.

                    [Afghanistan 2009]

After Otto Dix: 1891 – 1969
An Exhibition

WW I

It's said, in the aisles & alleys of the heart, he was driven to death crawling hand over hand through the mud & abandoned skulls from trench to trench to peel back the shredded skin from his comrade's head to see inside where the blood & gristle nestled, where the face without an eye or mouth or nose could be seen up close for what it was – a trifle launched to gamble with those who come from the other side, over the hills & into the valleys, wielding bayonets & mustard gas leaving behind skeletons still clutching guns & knives staggering from grave to grave too driven to stop too exhausted to die.

The Weimar Years

are littered with withered women & the bulbous men who hunt them. Their breasts are withered, their faces & fingers withered too. Where the sailors hunt the women are for sale & where the bankers hunt the women are robust & willing for a bigger price. The Weimar Years swagger in ties & tails & veils & plumes, they're noisy & naked & leave the dead to rot in their walk-up flats where the blood on the floor is sticky & scrawny dogs fuck in the cobwebbed corners. The Weimar Years spawn these hags with their filed tooth & baggy tits to swirl like irrelevant ghosts across their mirrored & lacquered rooms where the whiskey flows, the black night falls & the band plays on.

In Gallery Four

he's posed a fox like a panther to sever your heart & trash your bones.
& him, trussed in a tux, a naked woman on his lap. He strokes her
flabby breast & licks her ear. She smokes & stares into the void where
the old pros haggle for a quick date & a cat cracks a rat with its saw-
toothed bite. Dix is busy here & his collection growls & grows. He's
added an oil of the dancer Anita Berber with her sable wrap, pet monkey
& a silver brooch packed with cocaine & another, the desecration of
Flanders, where the dead float in stagnant pools & the living resemble
rotted stumps. Here are the heavy, well-worked hands of his parents, a
gaggle of lawyers dealing cards to empty chairs & the smoke & haze
that follows him like a shroud . . . sketch by sketch & stroke by agonizing
stroke.

Neue Gallery Space – New York – July 2010

Remembering Che Guevara

I've written about him & of his life as a 'revolutionary' if that is the proper word to identify a man or woman who fights for truth in the midst of lies, for freedom in the midst of oppression, for possibility in the midst of poverty . . . & lives or dies by those actions

My Response to Tyranny Is Often (without a weapon in hand) a Poem:

My brother-in-law used to care about the dispossessed. Today, he lionizes those who have achieved economic superiority & even fame.

1

Who will acknowledge 'The Other' in our midst?

*

*Blood in the mouths of those who must
grit their few sturdy teeth over fetid gums.*

*Blood in the eye of the drunk who guzzles
to forget – will die remembering.*

*Blood in the shit of those who eat
from the street & blood in the urine too.*

*

Che Guevara
took to the streets,
to the hills & to his death.

They made a mess of him in Bolivia.
One wanted a hand but landed
a finger.

One clambered for his head.
Settled for
a photo.

*

2

Think 'stone.' It too will erode in time.

There've been sightings of an Ivory-billed Woodpecker thought to be
extinct, sightings of a Highland Manga-bey Monkey too.

*

Where are the commandos in their lean & green?
Where are the lizard-men who never shrink from a good fight?

Here: In the jungle. On the plain. In the desert.
They hunt the butchers of the land & those who'd steal the seed.

They are few but, like the monkey & these exotic birds, if one can stand
there can be more
hidden
in caves & gullies, forests & ravines.

It's time.
Set-out a meal worthy of hope:
the mission
never abandoned
the mission
never
auctioned
away.

After the drawings & prints of Fernando Bryce*: An Exhibition.*

Fundacio Antoni Tapies - Barcelona, Spain.   2010

The Builders Of Bombs & Lies Connect Each Wire

1

After struggling through smoke & grit for most of the day, he finds an armored truck in place of his house. After scouring the grounds he realizes his family had been taken & there are no stars to keep him on his way.

2

He'd been carrying her dead baby most of the night when they appeared & motioned for him to follow. There were six of them passing a small black box back & forth & joking about mistakes & the dead they'd buried.

3

No one had been able to answer the question, how or when or how many, but when the bridge was crossed & the wires were strung it was too late to turn back.

4

The first man they encountered on their way pronounced them heroes & offered cigars & as they turned to leave he shot them both.

5

In the upstairs rooms with the famous portraits, tea service & connections to mayhem or providence no more than a click away, the chosen-ones practice a mantra no one must ever know & dare to challenge.

Coming Together

No one arrives before the summer fiesta.
It's an unspoken rule for those who
tamper with time.

We were the first, my devoted Emily & I &
our suitcase that's seen all you'd ever
hope to see of the world.

Caroline came next in a gauzy gown, impractical
for the beach, but she wears it well,
don't you think? & Oh Yes,

there was Arthur & his bombastic Ferrari &
Jules & Damien & Pookie with her bong,
black-tie & diamond nose ring.

The day broke well & after a beer in the blue &
orange bungalow, Simon doused us
with news of the war &

certainly it was Harold's time to die for his country &
he had & that's when the eight of us
straggled off, as always,

bound to the lies that brought us here & the lies
that will follow & so it is, as it always is . . .
donchaknow

After: Compania Nacional de Danza 2 – Barcelona
<u>Coming Together</u> – Coreogarfia Nacho Duato

Caravan

1

Inside we wager where

it's said, the Harem is the link from desert to the family home & dinner
that awaits the wealthy traveler. There's the separation of time

into hours & minutes & a theater of prizes for the dancer who plays the
tambourine for the soldiers who've come,

their bullets wrapped in lies, their visions of sisters rented to a prosperous
prince & the time to shake a hand all green.

It's here, in the fruits of conquest that truth be told: the politics of cunt
& country – resolution by supply & demand,

"You sell me hers & I'll surrender enough to pay your way."

2

At the oasis

the water's been poisoned & the guards who protect the relics &
hieroglyphs take no prisoners but remove the veils

from the brides & mount them & their horses & ride to the famous iron
gate where no one passes twice & . . . & here

the captain riddles the locks & hurls insults at the eunuchs & one by
one the selected are set free &

roam at will until they're called to play the flute for his highness & his
many whores, wives, concubines & sons &

it's then the bath is drawn & the President is called to pick a number &
couples dance in time to the drum & bugle & fife &

here the false prophet reads from the book & orders his caravan to
begin the long trek back to another time

when there was still a safe & sacred place & the family was whole &
could dream of a cautious if tentative peace.

After: The Chris Higgins' trio @ Club Bel Luna – Barcelona, Spain
& An Exposition: 'The Harem' an investigation – CCCB

At The Entrance / The Neon Pleads "Keep Me Safe"

One crippled hand trails another & nowhere to turn but toward the wall bearing the memories of a simpler life:

Up close, he's offered images of the bristles that encircle the body's tender holes. Before the door to the attic, he's scribbled:

Ignorance, Wrath, Desire / Panic, Anxiety, Hysteria / Hunger, Insomnia, Disease:

&

To assimilate you must: lighten your skin / straighten your hair / practice to enhance your orgasm

*

In Technicolor, framed across the opposing wall, a blue baby born in a rank motel / a woman rocking the dead thing in her blood-red arms.

*

A riot begins in Kandahar where men & boys fight over the stoning of a woman.

*

A Vietnamese family weaves (14 hours a day) baskets & cane chairs for markets in Lima, San Palo, Paris & San Francisco.

*

The final image is that of a porcelain toilet planted beside a cabin in the woods & evokes a loud & uncomfortable snicker from the visiting class, followed by instructions before a colon exam: *lie on your side, insert the nozzle in your rectum, squeeze the ball slowly, water will flow*. Relax.

It will be over soon.

After: The Exhibition "Disquieted" – Portland Art Museum – April 2010

The Sculpted Visions Of Olafur Eliasson

[As The Iraq War Enfolds]

I walk across this field of cinders & ash & through his mirrored passage
all tilted & fractured, into the room that swims in smoke &

here I lie on the bed that maps the course of time & place & dream of
the thick-lipped vagina in the tree that has been torched & its skin
peeled back &

wait for word of the other mutations & mutilations that mount as the
day grows colder & death waits in the wings like a pale bird crouched
on the lawn

where I wake to the seductive whispers of a woman in a yellow blouse
with a camera who's come to freeze this trance in time . . . But – there
is no way

to capture what will not wait as the tanks come faster & the drone of
the planes grows louder & the bombs & the fires,

that attend that moment, break the will of the sculptor who wanders
from room to room with his chisel & broom &

fills the bath with iodine & swims out where there are no hooks & the
fish are free & the mermaid in green

is all he will ever remember of that day

Madrid, Spain

For Judy

A Father's Lament

I scale Mount Moriah but my son is not with me.
I've come, once again, to bear witness,
To what has been done, to what had not been done.

My steps are heavy. My steps are small. I hear his laughter,
his music & his words – as he left them. Touchstones
for us to contemplate among these crags & shrubs.

My tears light my way – shimmering – step by step.
I was too late to the task as was commanded, blind
to the lamb that stood in place.

Only shards & embers remain. My knife is sheathed.
Who will settle my account? Who will hear my prayers?
I scale Mount Moriah but my son is not with me.

After: Some thought of Asher Klatchko

Contraband

*The arrogant fall through white water & the tip of the mast is all
that remains.*

It takes no more than a butcher & a cook to make ready the next meal
& of course, there's the willingness to run alongside & wave at the sick
& naïve who've come to answer the Governor's call.

'Shush' (as in a dream):

"It'll be a moment you'll least expect:

The hero among us will rise up & say, 'No!'

& the weary & enraged will know

there's opportunity & someone sane"

This they'll whisper in their shops & bars, behind their fences, in back-
rooms & front-rooms, even in the streets where the bodies wait to be
buried

ᾰ . . . ᾰ

Who will chart the rhythms of those who still wander &

Who will wash away the blood?

&

Who will track the lost who willingly marched &

Who will bury the last to die?

&

Who will tell what must be told?

Haunted

There are men & women who cannot see the sun rise without suffering a crippling pain between their eyes . . . those who fear the ticking of a clock.

*

An out-of-work carpenter in Sicily sets himself on fire on the steps of the Palermo Municipal Courthouse. His note reads: *I am ruined.*

Dimitris Papadopoulos, a recently laid-off insurance exec in Athens Greece, shoots dead his two kids, his wife & himself.

*

Where there's a garden in full flower, some see only the falling petals – a viper where a young kid pirouettes & prances.

*

Andreu Font, a Spanish geology professor who lost his job when his college was forced to close, hangs himself from a mid-town lamp post.

In Toledo Ohio, in front of a glass factory where he once worked, Robert Hall props the muzzle of a 12-gauge under his chin & pulls the trigger.

*

Where the mountains meet the sea, there are those who dread the untamable rage of the catapulting surf – the tranquility of the receding waves.

*

On May 25, 2011, Fay Yee calls her neighbor to ask her to look after her Collie pup then leaps to her death from the Golden Gate Bridge.

*

There are men & women who cannot see the sun rise without suffering a crippling pain between their eyes . . .

Emptiness Over Solitude / Expulsion Over Welcome

One day we're locked in each other's arms & the next, perhaps riding a mule up a steep hill or a tank over trenches. Or . . . bent

by the pale light reflected from the walls of this deserted museum with its relics from Mecca & Tokyo & Chicago:

cast off charms with names inscribed: To Yidzach from Marta, to Yin from Lu, to Jim from Becca / Or . . . stolen

moments intent on finding the right street that will take us to the river & a ship that only sails at midnight & still

we find no one to welcome us or help us map our solution. No.

We are the expelled & it's our turn to rescue order from chaos, our place

to find another way.

After: Sergio Belinchon's – <u>Ciudad</u>

George Crumb – Makrokosmos
I – II – III

Makrokosmos I

Out of the mist – Out of the thunder – Out of the rain. Here we go & Here we come – Shazam & Wham & the boldest among them flings a spear or is it a hook & ladder – barrage – build – break-down. "Once upon a time . . ." & – Where were you when the kids were snatched & where were you when they torched the forests & one by one & two by two & the river rises & the waves explode ten miles inland & here he's injected fluttering wings & titillated monkeys & a trip to the country with Uncle Bill & Aunt Rose & Mom & the Model of Certitude & Finesse & Twinkle-Twinkle & let's all join in. & There's much to discuss & where in hell are the symbols & there's a dead body at the top of the mountain & buzzards & gawkers & a woman's scream & in the distance a stream & a fly-rod & coconuts & we tip-toe through-the-tulips & out on the grassy knoll a phantom gondolier prepares for the unseen journey – Burn Baby Burn screams the master of the Anatomical Amazon. One step at a time. Six already dead & hundreds locked in cages while their psyches fester & minds fracture & the whistler whistles & the robber robs & all is well with the plan to dismantle the planet – Coveralls & Scotch Tape & a Tiny bell & Ripped seams & Camouflage . . . Whisper & Wrangle & Who's to blame? & Why not? & bubble gum & Uncle Mike's moustache & they're at it again – One note at a time – Come my love – Deliver on those promises why doncha? Not so you'd notice. Not as planned. Not . . . The Abyss of Time, he said. & meant it. & here's where the fun begins. There's not much left. Drumroll – Circumstance. Her song is short. Sing it again. Tinker-tinker. Out of the rain. A little bird must fall. You're almost finished. Kaput. Finito. Done & Gone . . . Rattle & Weep. Bauble & Squeak. Rut & Strut. Butter & Bombs. Or so we thought. That was then & this is proudly foolish. Love is in the air. Dream no more . . . & with that I say, Yikes!

Makrokosmos II

In spite of the first mistake. & then there were two. Enraptured. Infatuated. Get the big one. Yeah. You got it. Yeah. Wonder of wonders. Like a penny along the curb. Kids playing hopscotch. Mumbley-peg. & so it goes. There's rain in the forecast & a stop to make before . . . Listen! There she is. Both hands & rapping about her Midas Touch & who came the night before. Such tenderness. We could use more. & Then there's the walk among the wild onions & temperate musings. Open the book & remove page 6. Don't ask why & never tell. & Here – The pause is deafening. Twinkle-Twinkle. One step at a time. The stars align. Just so. Yes. I can feel it. That cosmological stuff. Those songs among the stars. One day at a time. & Now we know. They came to destroy & they're doing a pretty good job. A penny for your winking – thinking. No. It won't be long. Ever wonder why? I sure did. It was in the canyon. Yes. The one with the alabaster walls & that tidy bed. You remember. I Know. It was a long time ago. & a long way off. They'd been lovers or so they'd said. Harmony. Harmonics. Hair-Raising. Rubber boots. Bollywood. Bongo / Bongo. Boy. Was that sad. Slip it to me, baby. Like ripping up a seam. One note at a time. & then . . . Druids @ Stonehenge? Surely, You're kidding. I never said that. & No. I don't. &. For no other reason. WoW. WoW. Don't take it out on us. Where's the fire? Fire away. One good thing. It's not a cage. It has running water & a pencil sharpener. Quilts. Bitch. Don't ever be sayin . . . Ring-a-ding-ding. She's excited now. Hurry up. Tora! Tora! Tora! My ass. Is this what we worked for? All these shenanigans? We've entered the classical period. One word from him & it's Adios . . . A quaint concept. Like a bush on a plate. Beaver in a box. Badger. Ho-Hum. Squat. & Squat she did. Is it time for Tea? I'll have a Guinness. One by one they took a swig & the wall came tumbling down. & The drunken soldier swindled the little girl. It was Wednesday. There was very much at stake. Through the heart. What about the careening car? Elephant garlic? Romeo & Oscar Hammerstein? It was. Never like that. I don't know who told you. They were not always. Like a cosmic wind. Like super-duper. Who's that? Whistling? & Then it stopped & now we know. There's more to it than beefsteak & butterflies. Look out! She's got a knife. One thing after another. Major & Minor. Really? Unexpected? There's that knock on the door. Galactic bells. Water running. Fast current. Faster. & Then it stopped. Ramrod. Black Orpheus. Guadalcanal. It all rings true. Basket case. Bloodhounds. Balderdash. Ah, She sings again. Who will buy the bottle? & Tick-tock. Rock-Around-The-Clock. So tender she might break. The kids came running. School bell – Squeaky door – Sinking floor. There's a secret door. Behind the bookcase. Just like the movies. Time to put out the lights. Wait! I just arrived. Don't be upsetting the cart. You should know better. It's then the old man speaks. Summertime. Saskatchewan. Submarine. & So they went, hand in hand, up the steep & down the easy. What a wonder – What a damn fool. Those who speak of a god. What else is new. Under the sun. Ponder & Wonder. Udder nonsense. Moo& Moo& Moo& Moo. Running far ahead – The Lemur & The Leprechaun.

Makrokosmos III

Music For A Summer Evening

1

Wait – Hear it? Wait. There it is again. Wait. & Again. & Here & Now & There's that incessant droning in the backroom & flashes of fast & furious & fascination with Time & here. He is again & She with him & It's a quiet summer evening & There're others in the grove. Wait. A thrilling trill & Shush. &. A rattling in the willows. & The others have arrived & One at a time & Together they gather at the gong. &. It begins to move. Hear it. Hear them. Running over the unmown grass. Their pace quickens, an argument ensues. No disappointment. No anger or rage. Calm is organized & vigorous competition & shrill explosives. Hear the echo? Faint. Reverberations. & . . . Dazzling, isn't it?

2

On the wind. It comes toward us on the wind. The whistle. Pipes. & Piper. Like a lullaby. Coaxing. Cooing. All cuddles & quaint. Wait. They're dancing on the lake. Actually. Around the lake. His hand massaging her bare back & buttocks & . . . Hear it. Rumbling. In the distance. Don't stop now. It would be a shame. Wouldn't it? Of course. They come together. Hear it? The whistling stream? Reverberations. Dazzling.

3

Not doom. Mysterious. Someone's coming. Unknown. Uninvited. While Lovers abound. Clouds pass by. A hint of rain. Or is it. Thoughts of an uncertain future? Reach deep. Prepare yourselves. The air quickens. The ground seems to shiver. Calm. Calming. Play it honey. Do it to me.

Yes. Wait. There's more to come. &. Don't be surprised. He does that. It's his secret & he guards it well. Zip-Zip-Zip. There. He's done it again. There're only a few from so many. Where have they-all-gone. Wait. Maybe. They're following him. Up the hill or Out to sea. It's happened before. & Just when we've agreed. To begin again. Not Torment. No. Tumult? Only. Zip-Zip. See the kids & a suspicious skunk. At the edge of the meadow. Testing the dark.

4

Slowly. It rises slowly. He calls. To whomever will listen. A Name. He calls a name. Or is it a . . .? The Bell. Demands. We stop. Listen. &. Wait. It's a test of will – Or is it? There he is again. Mouthing platitudes? No. It's to entice. A shake of the shoulders – So to speak. & She answers with her staccato mumblings. I've waited so long & Now – He's back. The timbre of his voice – Its strength . . . As if by invitation – Some guests have returned to pay tribute – to recognize their advantages. The air is softer now. Harsh words set aside. For what will come – Or Not.

5

Bingo! & Bam & Pop-goes-the-weasel. Purity. From Chaos. They slowly turn – In each other's arms. Like marionettes. Like models of confusion – Peace & languor. The door opens. A love scene is being prepared. The grass is soft but loud. It calls for the naked to begin – Anew. Rumble – Rumble – Rumble. All for one & one . . .? To be measured. To be stuck in a bottle. To be freed from fear. Encouraged. To wonder. That Bell again. Open for him. Or is it her? Wait. A sweet breeze. Moon rocking slowly in its cradle. Talk to me darling. Make my night explode. Like last time. Yes. Like last time. Remember. & The applause is deafening. Rocking. Flexing. Fashioning. Clarity from circumstance. Touch me there. Yes. & May I touch too & There too & Oh my. My. My? You can almost. Remember now. All you needed was a little coaching. Right? I'm here to tell. Prompting. The voice in the trees grows fainter with the waning moon. It's as if someone has lowered a gauzy blanket over the scene. & There he is. Marking time. In his inimitably tender way. Hum along. Stay together. There will be more to come. Bong & Bong & Bong & . . . Twinkle-Twinkle. Night-Night. Sweet dreams. Night-Night. Sweet dreams. Night-Night.

Origins, Epiphanies & Reflections

Amid The Litter

her ashes, false tooth in a box & a note from the coroner: *Blood-alcohol through the roof.*   It's Sunday,

war continues, there's a Saint's game on TV, a skein of geese, dad's embossed cuff-links, squirrels fucking on the fence.

We'd met at the bank – fifteen years – This morning scrambled eggs with spinach, onions & shredded feta . . .

There're the dive-bags from Belize & her locked camera case, assorted photos:

Madrid & Venice, Paris & Prague, Amsterdam & Budapest. Time's stained her stuffed Raccoon – In one corner,

her Schwinn with those mismatched tires . . . In Dubrovnik, climbing in the rain over red tiled roofs, she'd vowed

to contend with living. New York was a safe place to drink – there was always company. Once, in the desert,

she'd found a nugget of pyrite: *Good luck, Energy, Stamina, Determination.* That night she dreamed of riding a stallion

over the mountains & into the sea, I could hear her urging him on . . . The Afghan carpet's been rolled & tied, books boxed

for Goodwill. With the last carton stacked, a pair of rats pause to eyeball the lot.

Collection will be a day early.

At My Desk

Listening to Bartok

1

There's the overdue bill from Macy's, stamps I promised to send Andreu,
the will I'll need to revise

now that she's gone – along with her *never-cared-much-or-often* kids.
Seemingly, there's no defense

against loss or is it change we fear? Last week my desk was clean,
rent paid & her picture moved

to the dresser drawer. Today, as if by magic, she's insinuated herself
once more & chaos reigns.

2

I'm listening to Bartok's 3rd piano concerto & polishing this glossy frog
that will be a paperweight.

Order is a sick elephant. The teapot dares test my courage. The rusty
knife from Vladivostok marries

the pearl-handled Lugar from Berlin. Even the Schnauzers are suspect,
even your voice changes

with the weather – just like you – it rises & falls, is flecked with blood
&

cannot hit high C.

What The Street Rendered

Crushed red cherries & a collapsed wooden chair, cartoon sketch of a naked man with one testicle, autumn leaves & a black pocket comb, an orange soccer ball, dried lilies on a fence & Q-tips, a blue plastic toothbrush, a fallen tree – sectioned & sawed – portable steel fencing & strands of striped police tape, a flowering Princess Tree, motorized wheelchair, bits of human hair & a miniature rubber duck, chain-links, a black suede shoe & a kid's white plastic raincoat, a jack hammer, stacked white plastic chairs, the signs: Tabac & Boulanger.

After: Jean-Luc Moulene: La Vige (The Lookout Man) Photos –
Paris, 2004 – 2011

Summers Fade To Fall . . .

There's the eternally surprising eruption of the Tulip tree's aptly named blossoms, the bellicose trumpet vine that erupts in a cacophony of wasps & bees, that tense but tender liaison with Jolene in the hayloft all mascara, semen & Eau de Toilette. There're walks along the lake where, at night, a gritty Egyptian carpet welcomes the couples who caress in its folds & ride it high to Cairo, Bagdad, or Babylon. There's Candy, Karen & Sofia, pinball, pinochle & Lucky Strikes. There's Cutty Sark, bloodstained sheets, smack & unrelenting crabs. There's the storm that tore the roof off, the fire that melted Doc's sugar shack, our sweaty ride to Daytona, that Triumph Tiger & snow in the Smokies. There're Highway Cops, 5-card stud, rigged roulette & Ruby – never forget Ruby. There're trucks with bullets, Band-Aids, Butterfingers & baby clothes. There're all-night-beers with Monty, eight-ball @ Jakes, Mary-Jane & the last dance with Caroline in Cicero. In the end, summer wistfully fades to fall & with it stiffening joints, whiter beard, a shot or two of Tanqueray @ 3 AM & maybe, if your luck holds out, that old breeder-dog her handler called, with a touch of hopeful irony, Jubilee.

From My Terrace

There's a blind brown dog sniffing along the gutter & a displaced Korean fisherman slicing a salmon.

There's a widow with a limp who smokes a home-rolled joint & a lean cyclist racing a freight to the crossing.

There's a cop with an unsheathed baton & a can of Coke / smoke from a fire on the second floor.

There's a swimmer wearing a mask & fins stroking through the smog & two teenage girls swapping stories of their first fuck . . . There's a balloon & a cat &

in due time, there'll be a conversation between the widow & the cop who lends his daughter to a passing preacher &

there'll be a rally to steady the rest of us for inevitable bouts of sabotage & hunger & there'll be no turning back from the edge . . . not this time – not any time soon.

November 2016

Swallows

He begins his walk at dawn with working-women, their mops & brooms &

"Bon Dia," says the Nigerian. "Bon Dia," says the grinning gypsy
wagging an accusing finger.

Above the square, feasting swallows swoop & swirl & sun spikes the
tiles &
litters the path with nuggets of applause.

"It's going to be hot," says the Scottish lawyer to his wife in front of the
 market where they buy yogurt & fresh peaches.

She squeezes her husband's hand & fluffs her loose blond hair. Their
brochures promise relics, romance & boundless recreation.

He doesn't have a brochure & cannot re-create what might have
been but is
no longer. His memory is tattered, what remains

is that last photo of his wife, a Colt Python, compliments of San
Francisco Health & Housing, glaring from her collapsed lap.

Even their past retreats & the allure of this seventh century refuge
could not slow her race to oblivion . . . Today

before a salt-encrusted cod & Viña Sol at Minerva's he'll hike the
castle's wall to the top. It's said,

if you make the climb, you'll be certain to return   refreshed & renewed.
It's a chance he's destined to take . . . once more.

Revisiting Tossa de Mar after thirteen Years – July 2014

His Fitful Sleep

There's a small wooden
heron poised on one leg planted
in stiff clay behind the house.

Where were you
when the bell rang &
the letter arrived?

Where were you
when the ship docked
& he arrived?

You've always relied
on coincidence
to bail you out.

Time to pony-up.
There's no brass-ring
in this neck-of-the-woods.

The first rule is laughter,
the second, a bowl
of steamed remorse.

The next time you flag
a movingvan remember
your mother & St Louis.
What was it the driver said?

"Careful what you wish for."
Was that it?

Or was it,
"Never go out at night
without your razor?"

Improvisation: After A Sleepless Week

There's a Starling on the ledge just outside your window. There's Buffalo Bill wrapped in a flowered quilt. There's a soccer ball, polka-dotted underwear & an orangutan sucking his sister's thumb. There's a whistle-stop, boulevards, busted banisters & men without women. There're honeymooners & bird shit, rendezvous & shrapnel, old guys, sweet peas, puppet-masters, Singapore, rabbis & rhubarb. There're houses where the lights stay on, a woman with a Cheetah on a leash, twin girls holding hands & modeling brassieres. There's a fat woman who sings "Amazing Grace" in the shower. There's an avalanche, your bitter mother's bitter bite, your eagerness to escape. There's a Porcupine, sunburn, butter, blackout & musical chairs. There's an armed robbery, truculence, translucence, a torch-singer & turbulence. There's olive oil, how-the-west-was-won & Monopoly. There's your insatiable appetite for attention, *gobbledygook & winter with black snow. There's his hovering mother-in-law & her wagging tongue. There's you: Trapped. Trembling. Timid. & Triangulated. There's trouble with Harry, a hot-to-trot widow & times when she chatters with her mouth full & torture. There's Simon who says, "How simple it would have been. & Will there be another chance?" There's wondering: How to say good-bye, How to ask the question? & What about Blood-letting? There're Band-Aids, hurricanes & High Wind in Tuscaloosa. It's then, you mount the tattered stage, singing & dancing & waving . . . Adios.*

Between A Rock . . .

It occurred to him late in the day. No, not an ordinary day. On this day, his father called from the grave & ordered him to burn his house to the ground, to move to Birmingham where Aunt Ethel lived. Aunt Ethel, mother's favorite sister, with money & a mortuary, who hated anyone fool enough to confront her wisdom or her sacred purpose. On arriving at Aunt Ethel's he received a call from his ex telling him his derelict son had vanished from prison & left a note saying he'd be looking for revenge & as soon as he found it there'd be hell to pay & Aunt Ethel, sweet as she was, didn't tolerate family quarrels or threats of any kind warning him she'd shoot the bastard if he came gunning for him or her or anyone close by & now you ask, what occurred to him that day & for the life of me I can't remember, thinking instead of the time he'd had in Atlantic City & how he took up with a dancer from some off-beat show & drove all day & night to a preacher in Canada who married them on the spot & how the dancer moved into his house with her mother & two teenage boys & how, after blackmail, armed robbery & the FBI, he settled the divorce for fifty grand & an old Mercedes convertible. As far as I know, not much has changed in his collapsing life unless you count his obsession with suicide as a quick & efficient way to the after-life or his recent flirtation with necrophilia – given his late night work at the mortuary. Let's face it, he shaves & bathes daily, looks for God, pays attention & where does it get him?

Snow

Snow blew in with its rabbit's foot & a dose of clap from the watchman's daughter. It worried grandma & charmed the pants off Robert who'd come to butter-up the cook & stayed through December. Snow, with its glass harmonica & soprano saxophone will not be hidden away & insists on equal time in the bathroom. It's never been determined where or when it might arrive. Snow bunnies & popcorn. What a movie it was! One thing led to another & there was no stopping the women with Uzis & the men who ran with them. No stopping, that is, until brother Frank arrived with his handy-dandy machine & sent them paddling furiously across the Milky Way with tails high & masks askew. Snow allows for conjecture. Instance: It wasn't enough for her to shovel past him in her spring-green jeans mouthing platitudes: *lovely day* & *invigorating isn't it* while he plodded like a Clydesdale muttering *Fuck you* & *stick it sweetie* when Snow showed its furious face &, much to his delight, a flock of deranged geese swooped down to carry her off reminding him, one last time, of their meeting that August afternoon & a romp in the neighbor's pool & then to bed in the guesthouse while the guests were sunning on the lawn. Too bad, he'd thought, she couldn't have stayed for another in the back seat of the taxi but there will be others or . . . Snow & the warmth of a bundled bear sleeping it off under the barn & Willy with his bad leg & rusty shovel harmonizing with the men from Terra Haute in the back of the old Ford 150 with Snow marking their every tuck & thrust, marching two by two, shoulder to shoulder or soaked in blood & scurrying between bodies broken & bodies torn . . . Snow wears warrior white, slips & slides trench to trench & truck to truck, won't be held accountable, demands mayhem & promises to return intact . . . After a long silence, it's come to this: In the last frame, freed from intermittent clouds, a hot sun shadows Snow across the valley, hand by hand & boot by boot, his grim jaw tensed, a tattered banner flapping overhead exclaims:

Ignore Inevitability. Freedom Abounds

flurries to resume by nightfall.

On The Balcony

The small woman dressed in green is not sure how to survive the allure she has for the man in black who has arrived late & takes the seat across from her where she slices her lamb & nibbles her potatoes but stumbles over her spinach & . . . & she knows he can't be trusted but has promised fidelity & now we see their walk on the beach & the entrance to her hotel & . . . & as they discover in the bed at the end of the hall, there are more than miles between them & . . . & he reminds her how the ticking clock is a friend, but she is silent & instead remembers her father on Mykonos who left her for a lover & her sometime-sister in New York & those hot afternoons in the attic where they'd explored each other & the neighbor's vigorous sons & how the past is a refuge & when the van comes to take her to the plane they each wave their relief & she folds herself into the rhythm of the road & he turns to the street & the shops & the woman in white who waits with her martini &

. . .

Between A Cypress & The Road

a man herds goats & sheep & olive trees from centuries past still bear
an abundance. In the distance a town or two & over a rise the Patron's
house & green fields & from a hill even dogs & someone riding or is it
another Cyprees bent in the wind & . . . & as you come nearer there
are other homes: those of the aunts who tend them & the grandma-ma
who will now be nursed & there's the corral & the barn where you first
discovered your need to be together & now you're close enough to see
the walls are no longer slick with a healthy skin of polished tile & the
roofs are patched with thatch & the windmill has one blade & a lone
man arrives & waves his scythe & gestures to the lawn at the back
where a fiesta is beginning & a young girl bends at the knee & offers
her hand & you step into the circle & remove your clothes as does she
& you dance as one & ignore the barking dogs & the bells of the
church & the odor of the burning & when she whispers your father's
name you know you've come too late & when you turn the sun has set
& all you see is the quickening river & a few lean stars & the still
tethered mule.

After a painting by Robert Michael Shaw: Tuscany, Italy

Sun Dazzles The White Walls

of the hotel across the street where a naked man & a naked woman embrace on a bed & as evidenced by their animation don't seem to notice or mind the fact their window is open to someone who may be watching & as clouds partially mute the glare of the sun, they're outlined even more precisely & now I've pulled a chair closer to the window & follow them as they explore each other's body with their practiced hands & lips & now he turns her so her back is facing me & I can see her long lean muscles & her shoulders & arms where they reach around him & the muscles of her hips as they contract as she pushes against him & now she opens her legs & lifts one across his body & I see the hair between her legs where it glistens & as she adjusts herself to his entry he rolls on top & with his lips to her neck & his left hand reaching down and behind her to spread the cleft in her muscular ass he finds a rhythm that seems to work for them both & as he slides in & out she lifts herself to him first slow then faster then slow again & they pause as he lifts his head & kisses her on her mouth & she reaches back with both hands to caress and softly squeeze his ass & now her legs go up along his sides & her knees bend over his back & her heels wrap around him as she pulls him close & . . . & the thinning light has begun to dim & I imagine them roused from their slim siesta by the cool afternoon breeze & the shy way she covers herself on her way to the bathroom & he in his robe & smoking a cigarette & she slipping on her flowered stockings & he his black dinner jacket & the tune she hums while over-hearing the news of a capture in Iraq & his kiss on her neck before the lights go out & they close the door.

Daybook Entry – December 14, 2013

Landscape & Meditation

". . . elegy and fury [may exist] side by side, beauty and the heart of darkness sharing one language." Margo Jefferson

"Though I walk through the valley of the shadow of death I will fear no evil . . ."

These flat blue plains / a puzzle to be solved / each stroke or thrust or swirl another branch / another tree / another field crossed . . . The eye struggles for a root, a hand to squeeze as our feet slip away & we drown in the orange or green maze or the black & purple lagoon.

Early on, she eased into a neighbor's lake – all gray & white & tinged with ochre & a pale blue haze / Like tears her paint & like paint her tears – layer on layer – don't be afraid of summer in the valley – don't expect her to return & lead you to her room or to her bed – No.

Her challenge grows with each trip to the village for flowers or the city for wine. Her empty fingers flex each sleepless night as she circles her twenty feet of space – slashing out with palette knife & thumb & now her hands tease a red mouth open & fill it with two white owls & one dove.

From her Paris window a skiff sails past all pink & gold & the dark oarsman with the black beard cuffs the water & curses the heat & nods to where she waits in the shadows her hand raised & ready to strike at just the precise moment – ready to scatter her ashes on the empty plain.

After the paintings of Joan Mitchell – The Whitney Museum

New York City

Sequestered

After: Louise Bourgeois

1

They have her boxed in. Last room in the attic. She's not complained.

The remaining rooms tremble at the suggestion of bare & barred windows.

When she's had enough, she slips her chains & navigates inside the walls.

In the night, needing sustenance, she maneuvers to the master's bedroom.

Like the cocoon or carapace, skin is suspect, protection or perdition.

You hope she will not – but she must: *As his body turns in the dark .
. .*

2

The ox hip she's hung in the governor's lobby cannot begin to feed the soldiers he's conscripted to intimidate the maimed & dying, the hunters he's hired to slaughter the herds or the opium dealers he's recruited to lift the spirits of hookers, pimps & preachers alike – long live the three-legged ox.

3

Behind the scenes, you'll not find her available for interviews or video documentaries.

Those who know her will attest: she's never denied the timid, the tortured, or the brutally battered.

4

Fearless – is an epithet she's loath to wear. When cornered or insulted, *her chiseled fist* flogs her rage.

The Black Widow is her pet; Anger her lover – *Only visiting,* she says.

Avoid toleration, she says . . . & never ask it.

My space is sacred. Its inhabitants are sacred. I will protect it & them with my righteous eye.

Don't dare me. You'll not succeed.

    Power is mine . . .

An Exhibition – Dia – Beacon, New York

Mother Says

when the wind is high & the moon is dark you'll come to this place to wait for the woman in the blue hat who carries your disguise.

If you disobey, there will be men & they'll demand an offering & if you don't comply they'll take it by force & leave you without honor.

In the coming weeks, assuming rain & a sticky ride in the Major's limousine, there'll be questions you must prepare to answer.

In June, there'll be a sign in the morning sky – you're expected to comply & sing each note as would a cherished dove.

It's then, the one in the blue hat will return & dress you for your encounter with *she-who-waits-in-the-wings* who will teach you the laws of allegiance.

By December you'll be ready, muscles firm & reactions swift. Go willingly. This is the time of wisdom – The end of folly.

Ask De Kooning

Was it a lover's wet mouth (all those white teeth) that first enticed paint to canvas, her tongue licking at the edge, like a cobra flickering?

Or – Not that mouth at all. Maybe the secret one he'd found between her legs that day in early June when they were twelve & wanting, the one discovered

but unexplored, that innocent adolescent quim, the one he'll construct & deconstruct, sometimes slashing, palette by palette, while it snickered that crazy, sweaty,

elastic laugh as only a forbidden mouth can . . . Or – could it be a memory of the lips through which he'd passed at birth, Aunt Berta's temptation at sixteen, that last fling

in Rotterdam? Who can know – who can ever know? So – the models came & went, like a rosy proposition, a little more open, a little more moist, a little more willing . . . Each

fanning the musk of memory, stroke by urgent stroke, he'd flirt, on the cusp of a dream, sometimes enraged, sometimes sublime

where the fearful woman waits.

After: Willem De Kooning: A Retrospective – MOMA New York City,
NY

January 23rd 2013

Remembering John Logan: 1923 / 1987

This morning, while listening to The Writer's Almanac, I was reminded today's your birthday &

had you not, broken of body, will & spirit, chosen death, you'd be a worn & weathered ninety.

Keeler read a small piece of your poem *Believe It* & I remembered reading it aloud, at one of those memorials we held each year.

It was hard to see you die so slowly, bound to your bed, twitching for a way out until you finally found it.

They don't teach your work in the academy – not yet – but they will, resurrect those deft rhythms & surprising rhymes,

that romantic love of language you married to your relentless search for the perfect lyric, each a signpost

along your sometimes-rutted road from Red Oak to South Bend, to San Francisco to Paris to . . . You made your world jump

in our mind's eye, not like a barbarian tearing at the gates but as a lover opening the door to the potential of the heart.

When, as would be fair, they find you again, they'll have to hone a language

worthy of the peace you cultivated as only a naïf can.

Because you were – without guile, without pretense, without deception, as

careless of your safety as you were

your dignity at home. The street enticed & you responded, stumbling back

in morning light,

aware of the risks but unwilling to detour your course. & so it went until

the end – you, shattered on the sidewalk

fronting your old Bush Street address, your death as distinctive & private as

were your nightly rounds.

Poetry magazine calls you a major lyric poet of your generation

No one would argue. Only. You knew the rest. Told it so well:

"There is something grotesque growing in me I cannot tell. It has been

waxing, burgeoning, for a long time . . ."

It too, that thing growing, is gone, as are, in the end, all our secrets. Still,

the poems remain – fitting. The best left, the rest dispersed

among the rocks & waves along the Big Sur Coast – a favorite spot,

Partington Cove – The Smuggler's Cave.

There were 'the best of times' . . . the worst were yet to come. I'll remember

them both: the whole & all its intricate, eccentric & fractured parts.

Vagabond

After: <u>U.S.A.</u> by John Dos Passos – An Homage*

"The young man waits at the edge of the concrete, with one hand he grips a [well] rubbed suitcase of phony leather, the other hand almost making a fist, thumb up . . . the wind of cars passing ruffles his hair, slaps grit in his face." j d p (U.S.A)

His first hitch would be a train & its darkened cars jammed full of unwashed men on the move & they would fade into the backstreets of Baltimore & St. Louis & Denver like lice in a dog's scruffy coat . . . &

there would be a picket line & men & women chilled & men & women & kids dodging trucks & gangs of hungry scabs & cops & "Gitbackyascum!" & "Upyurass" & "Eatsheet" & "Fuckyurmother!" &

it was 1918 & on the front lines, smoke & rain & the stench of rotting human flesh & gas that scorched the eyes & what were we doin' here anyways & who sent us & where are they now & why . . . &

there'd be a meeting in a walnut-paneled office in New York or Detroit or Chicago & there'd be starched white shirts & cocktails & lawyers with contracts & a gold pen to hold & a line to sign on & money would rain down like ruby chips on the roofs of Pierce Arrow cars & fall too . . . as soft as snow . . . &

there'd be the hospital room & the body on the bed would be stretched on wires & the medicine would be morphine based & no one will remember who or what but there'd been horses & batons & they'd been warned . . .

"The punch in the jaw, the slam on the head with the nightstick . . . the big knee brought up sharp in the crotch . . . the walk out of town . . . to stand and wait . . . where the reek of ether and . . . gas melts into the silent grassy smell of the earth." j d p (U.S.A)

——

[When the bodies had been counted (here & there) & stacked (here & there) & the votes (too) had been counted & the mention (again & again) of 'change for the good of all men' had been said (again & again) & hours for work had been shortened & wages raised & prices too (of course), Dos Passos saw the door that he wanted open begin to close & after his first crop of apples had been harvested he left the salvation of the working-poor to others & planted peaches for the next year & pears for the next & cherries.]

——

* John Dos Passos was raised with money & connections to the right schools but, in spite of that background, he grew to resent the rich & their manipulation of the working people for private economic gain and how the power of money over men was ripping apart the egalitarian fabric, both social & psychological, that was the original hope of the founders of the country. Still, by the end of WWII he also came to detest the charlatans who tried to organize & subsequently manipulate the workingmen & workingwomen for their own political gain.

My Father Would Be 110 Today

Listening to Ursula Oppen's piano rendering of 36 variations by Frederic Rzewski

on a Chilean Song: *El Pueblo Unido Jamas Sera Vencido*:

The People United Will Never Be Defeated

I'm reminded of so many untested political possibilities & for some bizarre, ironic reason, my father

for whom my planting of a pear & a peach tree may have been a long-neglected homage – as was naming: the pear for Zoe, the peach for Noa.

He did that, named trees he'd planted for me & for my son, Jason & now I plant & name them for my granddaughters & . . . I say,

ironic, because my father was a loner & didn't give much value to 'people united' as a political or social credo or at least one he would pursue.

The work he chose: solitary, brooding lawyer in his austere one-man office, the weekend farmer (full-time in retirement) speaks to that. As does the title

of one of his favorite books: <u>Five Acres And Independence</u> – a pocket edition from 1945 that rested on his nightstand as far back as memory.

He was an autocrat defending his hard-won turf, an absolutist who made no room in his personal life for compromise especially with his arrogant, hotheaded son, but did for clients & friends. Ours was a treacherous outing where hornets hovered & lions hissed warnings at every turn.

& now, that's passed & I'm no longer that angry, defensive kid, fearful of the master-of-the-house but an aging granddad measuring his own life

breath by precious breath. He would have been 110 today. Happy Birthday, Dad.

April 27, 2012

Woman Of The Woods

She appeared from the engulfing trees, bearing her burden,
determined to challenge what has been left
for her to discover.

Clothed in kinship with families of the forest, her isolation
speaks of independence / of separation
from what might be expected.

At first glance we're struck by her hands, large & tense,
straining against the very thing
she holds:

A snake? A crippled branch? Possibly a sentry,
arbiter of safety . . . Or, is it a spirit
bent on sacrifice.

She seems to wrestle with the risk something or someone
will come to challenge her dedication.
Some antiquated shame

has her bent, incites her hair to mask the geography of her face.
A disguise? Or, is it muffled pride, a reflection
of a sacred oath she's made?

Hers is a battle best fought alone. Should we name her Eve?
Is this our desire or is it that of the snake & his
indomitable resolve?

Surely, if there's sin to acknowledge it will not be committed
by this woman. Certainly,
Not this woman.

Inspired by a Sculpture by Maria Lago – Beacon, NY - 2021

There Are Mothers

wheeling buggies over hot coals, messengers high on blue smoke & tabloids greasing the gears of genocide. There's a father further down the boulevard dancing belly to belly with a boy in black who offers a chocolate kiss & hisses in his one good ear; his tongue a torch to light the way to heaven's gate. There's a mother practiced in cures for an ailing head but nothing for a heart awash in dread who worships at the door where a mouth delivers a basket of lies. This is no time to question authority, shutter your windows or leave in the dark. & yet, there are mothers huddled with children in the woods who barter themselves for a second chance. They're tough & they're wanton . . . between screams & whispers, they have & they will abide.

Escapades:

Selected Prose Poems

Once,

when asked to conduct the Sunday Choir, he borrowed his mother's wedding dress & his father's boots & made a hit with the boy soprano whose aunt owned the gallery where he'd first seen a print of *Guernica* & bought Rousseau's *The Snake Charmer* to flesh-out his collection of turtles & frogs & when they were quiet once more he tried Amazing Grace & When The Saints Come Marching In & ordered a salad with smoked salmon & a hard-boiled egg to encourage desire & a waffle with honey & almonds to assuage fear & when the moon was high & full he left the town he loved & flew to Paris & a rendezvous with a lover from his past who could always make him toe the line & collect his thoughts like a monkey studying Shakespeare or a cowboy whistling Dixie . . . when they did find him, as they often do, he was living in a tree-house on Madagascar whittling ponies from teak, teaching himself Russian & how to balance in one hand the ghost of Euripides riding a mule & humming the theme from 'Never On Sunday".

It's Easter

or is it Passover he couldn't be sure not caring much for either in a
serious way but then there was tradition to respect & a girlfriend who
loved ceremonies & pageants & rituals with good food & wine & singing
& dancing & a quick roll in the hay before & after & as clever as he
was he couldn't master the calendar & always missed his calling or
those who called & here it was the beginning of spring & no one had
invited him to celebrate or even attend either or both & when, with one
hand behind his back, he opened the door to his heart & stepped inside
just to be sure & when, with a song stuck like a bit between his teeth,
he knew better than ever that today was the only one worth remembering
& left his house & never looked back.

Interesting

as it may be to some – especially those with a horse in his stable or a dog on a leash – he never encouraged fraternizing with the help or the civil guard or even his mother who lived like a queen in his memory right beside the statue of his father that was covered with pigeon shit & never looked his way – No – not once did he let on he'd ever been to Seattle or Nashville or carried a concealed weapon or illegal drugs or a passport from Jamaica – No – when he left this time it would be to climb Kilimanjaro like his son & daughter-in-law but without the vomiting or so he said – & No – he knew better than to explain traveling in winter to anyone who hadn't – this time he'd take Boris the bulldog & his Colt .45 & wend his way south where continents divide & like those hearty pioneers before him he'll ransack all he finds / harness an army to do his bidding & without so much as a second glance – liquidate the rest.

I can't seem to find the key to the door

you'll need to open – not unlike the time I lost my father's car in a fog of alcohol & morphine after spending the evening with Barbara in her cozy flat in Chelsea, the one with phantom birds that flew free & dove like bombers scattering small packets of blue dye to mark their trail, sipping martinis & skin-popping M & letting her doodle on my chest with a razor while I caressed her ample breasts & recounted the time in Winnemucca when an Elk the size of a locomotive charged our jeep & tore right through the top with its perfect 14-point rack – Yes – & tonight is a mystery you'll not forget for its lack of color or candor – take your pick – it's that I'm missing something important – not always – but more often than not.

It's Wednesday

& the corner grocer has once again invited Marcos the elephant trainer to prepare a feast for the holiday & we're all invited just like the time before when Maria & Nancy strutted naked in the rain & Betsy proposed a nasty rendezvous with Harold's elegant valet & your kids began a food fight that ended when Irene was shot in the face by Bernard who had stolen his father's S & W .38 & was known to detest anyone with black curls & that included his mother who wrestled him to the ground but not before Irene's brother Jack shoved a bread knife between his ribs – But – this year will be different with grilled octopus all around & guards at every gate & two mixed cases of Rioja from Bilbao, beer from Finland & Grappa from Tuscany where they say this year's vintage will be sensational & we're all invited to Bob's gallery for his opening & a horse race where the loser must sleep with the mayor's wife & perform all the erotic acts she is known to demand & expects.

After her suicide

he gave his first prostitute a Tag Heuer watch for a blowjob & the next a puppy for the works & after a few more days of terror bought a ticket to Katmandu & borrowed a fellow passenger's identity allowing him to enter a dream of self-immolation from which he escaped; his skin the color of rust / missing his eyebrows, ears & right eye. When they found him wandering the hills above Florence he showed them how he could remove what was left of his head & replace it with another that resembled that of Orion The Hunter – in his hands the corpse of The Lizard God & in his mouth a tongue that could never again shape his defense or tell the truth.

The truth of the matter

tells of the time in Berlin when as a young girl she wandered from her home, caught a bus, a cold & married all on the same long night of which no one would speak or didn't until today when she arrived at the station bag in hand & baby in arms to witness the feeding & migration of the great white birds of her youth & the birth of the blues as played by her Uncle Hermann who had swum to safety across the channel an occasion marked by a green cross fixed to his forehead & a rabbit tethered to her every step.

If you look closely

her eyes are not as blue as the moon or as red as the sea she's birthed
from – No – she bears the scars of a youth gone mad & a butcher with
one good arm who taught her to mambo at ten & shimmy at twelve &
as the seasons turned she learned to mimic the tides & distance herself
from the town & the mountains that guarded the mysteries she'd teased
from her mother who had no hope left & fiddled & flirted with daddy's
shotgun still warm from the hunt he could never forget when his brother
of sixteen rounded the bend in the road & stopped a torrent of buckshot
with his chest.

The winter

of his eighteenth year saw him wrestling alligators in Florida where he'd gone to rescue his sister from opium & bad whiskey & eventually settled for a role as Satan in the local production of JB where he won the Golden Feather & a trip to Dallas where the real JB lived with his broken promises & a wife who cooked roadkill & smoked cornsilk & often recited the entire chapter of Revelations from memory like her mother & grandmother before her & now to him who played his part well with tail & horns / fouled breath & forked tongue that darted in & out between her parted lips as he'd been taught.

In November

his lover rises in his arms all wet & welcoming / not unlike the salmon & the elk drawn to their complete embrace / before the cold that waits / before spring when the passion for ripening will release again the green that feeds their undulation / their fornication / their joy at tampering with skin & all the hidden textures of their bodies / wrapped in each other's arms they slip into the day or night / oblivious of time / they celebrate their ardor / sublime & absolute.

In search of an alternative

the revered & wanton wander together into the dusk of a long summer
day bartering what is left of their bounty for a meager meal or water
from a gourd proffered by a withered hand between the bars & as if by
unmitigated design the sheriff tosses his own son into the mix / the one
with the squirrelly eye & wisp of beard who can't count or muster the
courage to say *No* & on they go into the night baying at the moon &
gathering speed until they are one long train slicing through the hills /
dancing to a piper they imagine worthy but will never let them leave . .
.

Each time he left her stranded

on her side of their marriage bed she'd cut a notch in her tongue &
secrete the blade in her memory with the others / buzzing like hornets
to startle the raider who wished again to strut his stuff / & she / no
more the thin-lipped servant / whips out a serrated hand to slice the air
between them leaving a bloody gash where the moon had been & again
to extract muscle bone & skin / the shell will remain / like the husk it is
/ no more amiable than a whistle on the wind or a broken promise left to
rot.

"Watch out,"

he said & disappeared into the crowd – "Nuts," she thought but later in the day when the big brown dog chased her down the alley & a man waited with a van & . . . & by the time they got to Tucson the last she remembered was the radio & a voice that said the border was closed & he encouraging her to dance *'in the light of the moon'* as it was full & when he took her in his arms & whirled her across the desert floor she gave herself to impulse & married him on the spot – for that night at least – & that's what he'd tell his friends in Harry's Bar until Sunday when she stormed the door & dazzled them with her footwork & backed him flailing into a night of no return when the lights went out & he'd never be seen again.

The blue cat

her aunt raised stalked him 'til twelve when he could fight like his father who'd died in a war & steal from the collection plate without retribution & the escape he made to Wyoming in his twentieth year & the bullet he took in the back & the bodies he'd buried & the days & nights in dank cells & her . . . all temper & teeth / the child she carried in a cat carrier & swung like a censer before she'd tossed it out & him in Chicago bearing the cut she'd made in his chest where his heart may have once found refuge.

After a lunch of greens & dark bread / after

your last kiss / the dream of falling ice / casting the first stone / after your blood on my hands / the sighing in the trees / your burial at sea / after Aunt Maude's cat / a letter to Sophia / the fire / the camps / after the silver moon / a quick ride to the last door / sounds of alarm / after a cut above the eye / the naked & the dead / lies / & more lies / after the trial / the smoke / the mirror / after . . . the resonance of your eternal rant.

The effect is quite nice

never mind you can't see. "Never could," your wife says. "Never will," your son writes from Sing-Sing where he's been these fourteen years waiting for you & your accordion-pleated heart that can't play the tunes it once did as you stutter & stammer waiting for the next train to Berlin where mother waits in the yard beside the church with brother Bob who huddles with arms crossed & teeth on fire remembering the whip you used, the dog you axed & the phrase "Fuck You All" exploding as it did from your chair & hurling it through the window as if in the midst of the war you lost bringing nothing but rented dreams to the family table – to never be salvaged, birthed or even found.

Today's the first

he'd heard of his mother's fear of the vermillion bats she's kept in a cage since birth. Today he'll marry his mistress & sail to Rio where birds of prey sing on the wing of a tall black god who haunts the hills with soldiers who weep & monkeys that tear them limb from limb. When she surfaces again mother removes her blouse to suckle the coyote who's been the master of her house since Ruben's death & through all that remains – their unrepentant guide.

She'd be 103 today

had not the snake invaded her leg, burst her juice & the juice of a thousand bees / That day she'd revived her engine & driven him mad for a caress like the ones that made her famous as guard of the jeweled cave as it was called in those days when we all had a taste for sake & sashimi & gamblers plied their trade up & down our street where she targeted the winners & stitched her initials to the loser's door . . . time was right she'd say & humming a catchy tune sliced success from the unsuspecting & gorged on the fruits of their labors.

Homage To A Widow

The Widow Fishes

Her worm wriggles between firm fingers but has no chance to deny the hook.

She's a tested adversary & sets her line just-so, coaxing it over her favorite *lucky-spot*.

There are large-mouth & small-mouth bass hovering in these coves, under the sunken stumps.

She knows their secret haunts, fished them with her husband, gone these last two years.

Tomorrow, she'll embark at dawn & chum the waters. There will be fish dancing &

he will take the first cast.

The Widow Welcomes Her Lover

She's cooked his favorite: a coq-a-vin with fresh morels it being spring & she alone.

He's cautious not to go too fast while she appropriately defends against pleasure.

They're keenly aware of the history that surrounds them in this marriage bed

Inhabited now by their heat & urgency – Which will be the first to break this bond &

tempt survival?

The Widow Wanders Into The Sea

There are jellyfish to consider, spiny urchins & the dreaded barracuda. She never hesitates.

There were nights & days where a bong filled with marijuana settled her nerves & days

he's been thrilled at a sunrise so radiant & warm, as they are in the tropics, it overcame

the certitude of death at work . . .Their days are measured one toke at a time.

The Widow Paints

a ladder to the stars or is it a crowd that crafts a castle of their bodies,
arm by knee by foot by . . .

& a tree blossoms & the face of a friend & an assault on blue & black
that tears at the heart & . . .

each stroke a commitment all painters make but this is her coming
home & the canvas is a camp

where the placement of the mines are unknown & the wells are poisoned
Or maybe not.

The Widow Attends A Lecture

He begins describing the last painting: mold oozing like sap from the entrails of the lumbering dog.

It's in the garden gallery outside his home in the trees & ends with a bang as the dog explodes.

These are not her favorite rites-of-passage. She's volunteered to teach here & welcomes the earnest

but not the forsaken. Like Kenny who posed for the drawing or Maryann who made it.

The Widow Worries About Her Kids

It's anxiety birthed by death. We understand that. Grief draws its own boundaries.

& here she tries to deny her own suffering while the kids begin their journey back.

Who can tell a mother not to rush to repair what cannot be repaired? There's no time.

Each will find a way in the forest & where there is a mountain –

It will be crossed as well.

The Widow Reads Into The Night

examining the philosophy of the heart the way a mariner sights her sextant.

What appears on the horizon does not always fit what she needs for the story's end.

In the next chapter, she finds grace in paired swans skimming the pond in search of a place to make love.

How is it, this late at night, swans still trill like trumpets & dance like fireflies?

The Widow Relishes Her Hours Alone

When the bells of the church clock strike 3 AM she senses a peace that approximates freedom.

The fat years & the lean are devoid of sap. A trip to the lake. Woodpeckers at noon. Loons at sunset.

Here she'll roll her dough across the floured tabletop to shape the loaf. It's a fruitful task

work & food – Sustenance . . . A place to begin to plant in the new bed that will be the future.

The Widow Visits Her Husband's Grave

She is not startled, has wiled him to come & holds the ladder for him to climb.

They talk of times only they can know / she weeps & he weeps for her but is stranded

in a mirage . . . no substance but that which memory plants & harvests & plants again.

Each day is impossible without the other to give it the shape it needs to be revived.

Each night is a misery without the other enunciating the proper phrase that is the signal

only they can hear.